BRITISH ROADS
CORNWALL
PAST AND PRESENT

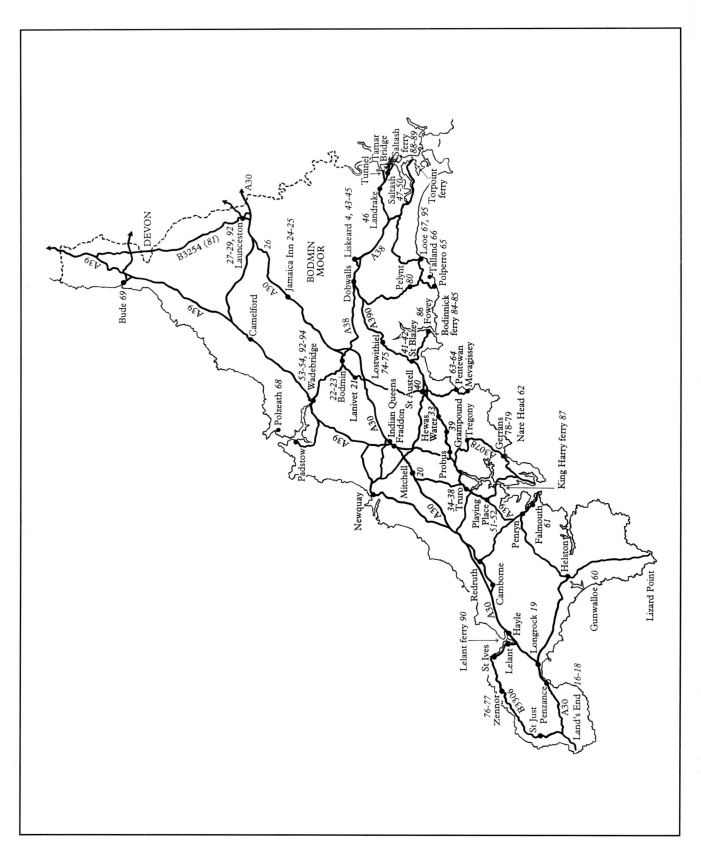

This map shows the county's major roads together with other routes and locations featured in the book. The numbers in *italics* refer to page numbers where the appropriate illustration may be found.

BRITISH ROADS
CORNWALL
PAST AND PRESENT

A nostalgic look at
the county's highways and byways

Valerie R. Belsey

'In retrospect, probably nothing that we had as children
was quite so important to us as our summer in Cornwall.
To go away to the end of England;
to have that bay, that sea . . . my father and mother gave me,
at any rate, something I think invaluable.'

(*Virginia Woolf*)

Past & Present Publishing Ltd

LISKEARD, THE PARADE: Knocking down buildings to make way for traffic has been a feature of highway history since time immemorial; records of the wholesale removal of such important premises as bakeries, black-smiths and pubs are found in the accounts of Turnpike Trusts throughout the country. What we see here in this 1958/9 photograph is the loss of the final half of the house in The Parade, Liskeard. This was where the local 'regeraters' held court, an office connected with setting the price of locally collected dairy produce and small game such as rabbits. The following signs were lost when this and the building behind it disappeared:

a The sign on the wall reading 'The Parade', probably manufactured from pressed steel.

b The cluster of pre-Worboys (pre-1963) signs, including one with a black and white checked top which denoted that the place named was the final destination if you followed further signs so marked. They read 'A38 PLYMOUTH', 'A390 TAVISTOCK' and 'B3254 LAUNCESTON', and were all provided by the RAC.

c The large sign at the bottom reads 'DEVON TRAFFIC: TO AVOID DELAYS AT TORPOINT FERRY GO VIA TAVISTOCK'. Today this might be advised as a more scenic rather than a quicker route. Why wasn't the Saltash Ferry recommended, I wonder?

The conduit in the square in the 1950s picture has been enhanced a little by the addition of the town arms to the Car Park sign, but the double lamp-post is uglier than the single one seen atop the conduit today. The whole question of attaching directional signs to existing monuments is a vexed one.

The 'past' photograph exhibits a particular absence of road markings; at the foot of the 'SHOPPING CENTRE & TOILETS' sign a group of granite setts have escaped the tarmacadam. During the Second World War the section of road in front of the Bank was laid with concrete to enable the safer movement of troop vehicles. Many of these aspects of highway history are dealt with in the following pages. *J. Rapson, courtesy of CCC/Author*

Contents

Bibliography

Berry, Colin *Portrait of Cornwall* (Hale 1963)
Betjeman, John *Shell Guide to Cornwall* (Faber 1935, Rev 1964)
Davidson, R. *Cornwall* (Batsford 1978)
Grigson, G. *Freedom of the Parish*
Halliday, F. E. *History of Cornwall* (Duckworth 1959)
Henderson, C. *Cornish Bridges*
Luck, Liz *South Cornish Harbours* (Nautical 1988)

Green Lanes Walks in South-East Cornwall (Crown Copyright, 1985)
Priestland, G. & V. *West of Hayle River* (Wildwood)
Rowse, A. L. *A Cornish Anthology* (Anthony Mott)
Todd *The Industrial Archaeology of Cornwall*
Trinick, M. Article on Nare Head (National Trust magazine 1985)
Scillonian, The Various editions of this fascinating journal

First published in April 1994

British Library Cataloguing in Publication Data

A catalogue record for this book is available from the British Library.

ISBN 1 85895 045 7

Past & Present Publishing Ltd
Unit 5
Home Farm Close
Church Street
Wadenhoe
Peterborough PE8 5TE
Tel/fax (0832) 720440

Printed and bound in Great Britain

Photographs credited 'CCC' are reproduced by courtesy of Cornwall County Council.

Map on page 2 drawn by Christina Siviter

Introduction and acknowledgements

'We are not going to do away with the great car economy.'

Margaret Thatcher, 1990

*I*n conversation with Cornwall's County Surveyor, Mr Peter Stethridge, the import of one of his statements in the light of the above quotation was heartening indeed. Unlike those who are busily planning the further destruction of the countryside in the South East of England with the proposed 14-lane widening of the M25, Mr Stethridge said that any major road works now taking place in the County of Cornwall must be right, as it will not be possible to repeat them. This means that if the doubling of traffic into Cornwall will not fit into the county, another way will have to be found for visitors and residents alike. So this book could be the last volume to be written on Cornwall's roads past and present!

It all begins with maps and novels. Whatever the time of day, whatever the weather, someone, somewhere in the British Isles will be opening up a map or reading a novel. And both have stories to tell. In the 'past and presenting' business the landscapes of the mind are just as important as the accuracy of the maps - the distinctiveness of every British county dictates this. What you, as reader, bring to a study of the 'past' photographs in this book is more than is actually there. If it is a familiar location, it will be full of the incidents and people you remember, and the moods that you associate with the place; sometimes people have spotted themselves or their old vehicles in the 'past' shots. Even if the scene is unknown, you will still recognise familiar lamp-posts, warning signs, Ford Anglias and bouffant hair-do's from your own life - just like a novel.

A volume of British Roads may have a theme prompted by a literary association that belongs to a past much older than 50 years:

'He walked up hill in the mire by the side of the mail, as the rest of the passengers did; not because they had the least relish for walking exercises, under the circumstances, but because the hill and the harness, and the mud, and the mail, were all so heavy, that the horses had three times already come to a stop, besides once drawing the coach across the road. . .

(Charles Dickens, *A Tale of Two Cities*, 1859)

Having read that, no one ever complains again about their electric windows not working! So it is often a feeling for a place taken from a writer's description that sends me running to 1960s AA Road Books or old itinerary sheets.

Then work begins on reading three or four histories of the county. These do not contain a great deal of information on roads as such, but by finding out about trade patterns, main rivers and ports, and important families and estates, a picture of communications throughout a county can be built up.

It is on the road itself that the writing really happens. No, I am neither a danger to traffic nor chauffeur-driven - just studying the landscape and watching out for clues to recent developments. Old fingerposts still standing, kerbing and modern lighting columns along an apparently rural road, the curved entrance to a layby off an A road with a faded white line off-centre - all clues as to how the road once ran, and why it has changed.

The 'motoring nostalgia' features are suggested by studying the county intensively. For example, in Devon it was fingerposts because of the great variety in the county with the highest mileage of roads. In Cornwall it was the discovery of a plaque on a wall in Redruth to Scotsman William Murdock, who invented coal gas for lighting in that town in 1792, that led to a feature on street lighting.

The acquisition of the photographs themselves depends on the helpfulness of individuals within a local highway authority, the chance road-based photo found in a museum or library collection, or a postcard or map found in a car boot sale. Then

ST AGNES (CORNWALL): The story of Cornwall's roads begins and ends with the sea, be it the A30 at Land's End itself or this twisting, leafy sunken lane at St Agnes on the wild Atlantic coast. *Author's collection*

BLOWING HOUSE, CAMBORNE: Little is said about Cornwall's industrial heritage in this book, since for the most part the county's mining activities were in decline by the 1920s. However, driving through south-east Cornwall, the furthest corners of Penwith and the central area around Camborne and Redruth, evidence of this industrial past is always in view. The chimneys on the extreme left of this 1975 photograph look down upon another era of industrial architecture.
Dept of Transport

once the 'present' photograph has been taken it is hard work with a magnifying glass that produces the text to accompany it. Having risked life and limb to take a photo from the identical spot - sometimes from the central reservation barrier of a dual carriageway - the resulting scenes often look less exciting than remembered!

'Blessed be St Enodoc, blessed be the wave,
Blessed be the springy turf, we pray, pray to thee.
Give to our children all the happy days you gave
To Ralph, Vasey, Alastair, Biddy, John and me.'
(From *Trebetherick* by John Betjeman)

Almost every travel book I have come across on Cornwall *ends* with a chapter on the Isles of Scilly. In this exploration of Cornwall's roads the Isles take pride of place at the beginning. During the course of the book we travel up from the almost motorcar-less Isles to the dual carriagewayed entries into Devon over the Tamar and via a tunnel. From light into darkness.

The story of Cornwall's roads must begin and end with the sea. Because Brunel's crossing of the great divide, the River Tamar, in 1859 has been with us for more than four generations, it is difficult for us to believe all those stories of going into a foreign country, of needing a passport when you go into Cornwall. Yes, it is a long way down (from London), but not really inaccessible. And who is to blame or to thank for that - not the Great Western Railway, but Henry Ford.

The story of Cornwall's roads has been much influenced by the sea. It is a narrow county varying from 8 km to 72 km in width and measuring 132 km in length, so you are never far from the sea if you want to be - as is the case with most visitors and residents. Even in the beginning the pre-Roman tinners did not make roads as such to take their minerals to the sea for export. The ridgeways in Cornwall peter out mysteriously in the areas where you think they might be needed most.

Its rivers, too, when not being silted up by the tinners, were important means of communication. Truro, the county town, was a seaport long before it became the ecclesiastical and administrative centre it is today. It is unfortunately beyond the time scale of this book to cover the early days of tourism and the history of the GWR's connecting bus services from main-line stations to remote popular holiday venues. But we can look at changing patterns of holidaymaking that have shaped the road system - the need for quicker access to Cornwall as a holiday mecca, and the need for better access to 'honeypots' historic as well as hot. Although mining is no longer the main industry, it too has shaped the road pattern today, together with quarrying. Centres of administration and commerce have also done this.

So without further ado let us start the story further out than the end of the land itself.

I would like to thank the following for their help with text and photographs:

Cornwall County Council Highways and Transportation, particularly Mr Stethridge, the County Surveyor, Mr Mogford from Redruth, and Mr Saville from County Hall.

The staff of the Cornish Studies Library, the West Country Studies Library, the Royal Institute of Cornwall, the Isles of Scilly Museum, Liskeard Town Museum and the Penzance Museum, and Liz Luck of the National Trust.

Elayne Downing from the TSW Film and Television Archive, Plymouth.

Alan Cooper Laboratories, Kingsteignton.

The Rambler's Association, the YHA, Haldo Bollards, Sugg Street Lighting and the Land's End and John O'Groats Company.

I would also like to thank the following individuals: Mrs D. Dingle, Mr M. Hawkins, Mr F. Gibson, and Mr Rapson.

Apologies to anyone not mentioned in the list!

1. The Isles of Scilly:
the beginning and the end

'In the end the path - the islanders call it the "road" because they built it - led nowhere. It buried its nose under the salty sand beside the church.'

Leslie Thomas, *Some Lovely Islands,* 1968

I have yet to find a book about Cornwall that sees fit to put the Isles of Scilly in the forefront of its proceedings. Understandably enough, this group of islands, now given over almost entirely to tourism, presents a microcosm of highway history and how it developed despite the sea.

Sailing into the Roadstead of St Mary's harbour up until the 1920s you would have been greeted by donkeys ready to carry your luggage to your hotel; they were the main form of transport, hence the early postcards showing the 'two Scilly asses'. Like the donkeys in Clovelly, no longer used for transport to and from the sea, their disappearance shows a shift in emphasis from sea-based communications to land and latterly to air.

Up until the 1940s the islands' roads were made up of water-bound stones using clay and local granite; remnants of these granite-bouldered paved ways can be seen along the edges of the Parade in St Mary's where the tarmac is wearing thin. Despite the abundance of local granite in 1947 there is a record of 500 tons of Newlyn roadstone being brought in to St Mary's at the start of their major road-building programme.

With the dedication of the 5-mile perimeter road round St Mary's in 1966 such phenomena as a 15-year-old boy driving a tractor without a licence would no longer be possible. The Department of Transport numbered the roads, which were to be maintained, giving them A status as the map shows. Although motor traffic on St Mary's has increased considerably, the coming of the mountain-bike-hire age for tourists renders the silent approach of whirring wheels more dangerous in some cases than the chug of tractors still bearing the original 'SCY' registration numbers.

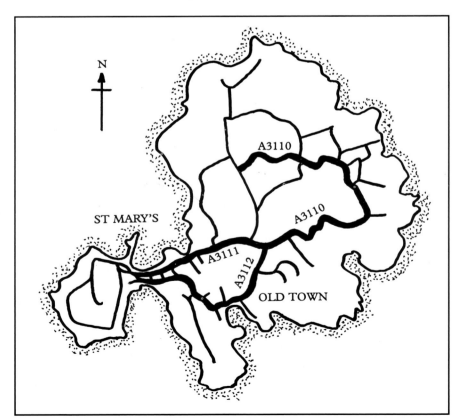

Left **Map showing the A roads created on St Mary's in 1966.**

Right **ST MARY'S (1): The historic telegraph pole in these photographs of Hugh Town marks the boundary of property owned by the Duchy of Cornwall on the island. Here the unlicensed vehicles are parked within Duchy land in 1969, before the introduction of Road Tax in 1970. When they finally had to pay tax the Islanders were given a special privilege, but as this extract from *The Scillonian* reports it wasn't received with any great delight: 'There was sarcastic laughter when part of the Ministry's letter was read out stating that it was felt that islanders might like registration letters which they could look upon as their own. The letter suggested SCY as being very suitable.'**

You will have to search today for the original payers of the first £25 levied on Island motorists who could not be saved by the pole. At one time during this trouble a white line was actually drawn across the road - early road markings for the Islands! *TSW Archive/Frank Gibson*

ST MARY'S (2): Saved from the sea! This area of St Mary's is best reached by either walking through the nature trail that runs from Porthmellon to Old Town, or by walking along the headland from the main town toward Old Town church which looks over to the scene pictured here.

There is a famous series of photographs taken by the Isles of Scilly's most important photographer, Frank Gibson, in Victorian times which shows workers moving huge boulders to build up the wall around the church. Maybe ancestors of those involved are inspecting the damage in this 1962 picture, where some of the boulders have been washed right up over the road in a storm.

The breakwater, defensive wall and new raised section of road (note the join in the surface) were consequently built; the cafe on the left followed later. Note the sad necessity of a 'REDUCE SPEED NOW' sign. Sections of the original stone wall are still visible by the small door-like recess to the left of the old bench. This is an unusual piece of stone walling for the Islands, where sweet-smelling Escallonia hedges are more common. These photographs were also taken by a Frank Gibson. *Both Frank Gibson*

ST AGNES: Prior to the use of concrete on the Islands, other road-making methods such as those described by the Aldridge's of Grinlinton Farm had been used for centuries:

'Maurice and Michael laid a foundation of large stones (which are never in short supply on a rocky island), then put on a surface of ram, which they hacked with picks and much effort from the thyme carpeted, gorse-rimmed pit on our downs. Ram is a special kind of earth that has a natural binding quality.' (From *Hobnails and Seaboots*, W. Aldridge, Harrap 1956)

Thus is described a timeless method of roadmaking that you will still find in use throughout the world.

But in 1955 on St Agnes a roadmaking revolution had taken place - the present-day photograph shows the new concrete road now in its 38th year and in need of some repairs in places.

The third view shows the Islanders working on the concrete road in 1955, and is typical of islanders' co-operation when a job needs to be done. Other islanders on other islands approached the task in a different way, starting simultaneously at either end rather than working from one end to the other as at St Agnes. Next time you are over there have a look out for immortalised footprints of the kind seen in the ruins of Pompeii! *Michael Currer Briggs/Author/Frank Gibson*

From farmyard to flyover

We all know of a farm track that has been made passable by the miraculous application of concrete, indeed, since the 1900s the use of concrete in road construction has been common throughout the world, especially in the Commonwealth countries. It is a cheap and efficient system and has produced some interesting and lasting effects, as the accompanying photographs show, illustrating both the early sandwich system and the reinforced steel type of concrete road. In the 1950s and '60s 'leanmix' concrete was in use - graded stone aggregate mixed with concrete. During the oil crisis years of the 1970s concrete was used more extensively.

As far as the motorist is concerned one of the problems caused by concrete roads is the lack of smoothness of the ride. However, the 'hard ride' feeling associated with all concrete roads finished transversely is virtually absent where the longitudinal finishing machine has been applied. Another problem is the noise factor, which seems to increase once the motorist hits a concrete road.

Concrete roads were built in the 1940s and '50s wherever new housing estates were springing up in the suburbs of our large towns. It is not the most attractive-looking road building substance, its whiteness being rather harsh. However, along Torquay seafront there lies some rather attractive pink concrete road resulting from the concrete having been mixed with red pigment.

One of the most famous and longest stretches of concrete road is to be found on the Southend Arterial Road (the A127) in Essex. Some 30 miles of the northbound carriageway were built by hand in the 1930s, although plans had been ready to bring in a mechanical laying plant from Germany until the political climate prevented it. The completed stretch remained the longest section of concrete dual carriageway in England until the opening of the second length of the M1 in the 1960s.

Here is an extract from a rousing pamphlet extolling the virtues of concrete roads in Britain:

'Every mile laid down uses British cement, and local gravel, stone and sand supplies - every order spreads employment through our coal and steel industries.

Cement-bound road at Brill: This was constructed for Buckinghamshire CC in the 1930s and, despite its linear appearance, was constructed in half widths on a steep gradient leading into the village. *Cement & Concrete Association*

Concrete was used throughout England, and this photograph shows a concrete road in the industrial North constructed over what was once a granite sett base. Is the little heap of identifiable remains on the left of the road evidence of horse-drawn transport still in existence here at Rawtenstall, Lancs? *Cement & Concrete Association*

This illustration shows the four principal stages in the construction of cement-bound 'sandwich system' laying. In the foreground the first layer of stone has been spread, then the layer of mortar, followed by the second layer of stone. In the background, the whole is being rolled into consolidation. *Cement & Concrete Association*

Reinforced concrete. This photograph shows the method adopted by Huntingdon County Council for widening main roads. The use of rapid-hardening cement for this class of work ensures rapidity of construction combined with minimum of interference of traffic. The reinforcement used is square twisted mild steel bars; other patterns were also used, triangular and rectangular. Other materials used in conjunction with concrete have included the laying of sheets of moisture-proof polythene on the M2 in 1962. *Cement & Concrete Association*

From farmyard to flyover

This photograph of the Swanley by-pass in about 1970 clearly shows the sections of concrete road shining in the sun. Interestingly enough Kent no longer uses concrete in its road construction programmes.

Note, incidentally, the nice selection of largely British-made cars in evidence - Fords, Austins, Morrises, with a solitary Renault in the centre lane foreground. *John Topham Picture Library*

2. 'The longest lane in England':
the A30 from toe to thigh

'The motor car has made the greatest change of all. Roads have been widened, blocks of houses have been taken down in picturesque ports to make way for car parks; petrol stations proliferate; huge hoardings to attract the motorist line the entrances to towns.'

John Betjeman, Introduction to *The Shell Guide to Cornwall*, 1964, first published 1935

As we have started from the Far West with the Isles of Scilly, let us continue this direction of discovery by following the main spinal route through Cornwall and attempt the impossible by landing at Land's End. Standing here

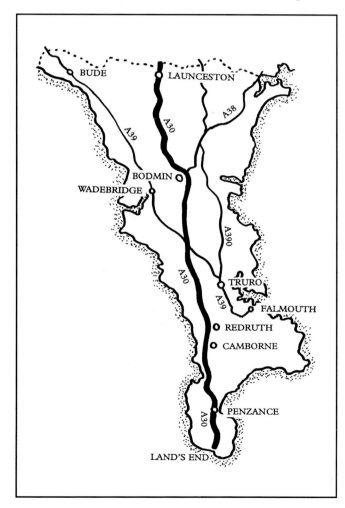

The A30, Cornwall's spine.

we see that we are 291 miles from London. With your Cornish guide book in your hand you can ask 'Pes myll der eus a lemma de Londres?' In Cornish, of course, because this must surely be a stronghold of Cornish nationalism, even if it is privately owned.

In Truro Cathedral there is a wonderful painting, 'Land of Saints' by John Miller. It shows the sun setting in the west and a band of Celtic saints arriving out of the darkness in the enlightenment of the Gospel. And it is with the Church that the answer to the central route through Cornwall over the moor lies - after all, a seabound route would seem more appropriate - when the removal of St Petroc's bones from Padstow to Bodmin made this moor-bound town the capital of Cornwall in the middle of the Sixth Century.

Here at Land's End, instead of standing looking out to sea, think of the 300 or so miles that you can travel along the A30, up through Cornwall to Launceston, to Devon through Okehampton and Exeter, to Somerset via Chard, Crewkerne and Yeovil. On into Devizes, Sherborne and Salisbury, and ever closer to the capital via Stockbridge, Basingstoke and Staines. The straight and stony Roman way then merges with what was to become the A4, later the M4, in Hounslow. Here was where the Great South West Road began, one of the longest roads in England and once the haunt of Dick Turpin and Claude Duval, where 2,000 posthorses were kept and the road was lined with gibbets to warn highwaymen of their impending punishment. A grizzly image, and far off in time and distance from what we shall see along the A30 in Cornwall today.

The cover of the February 1983 pamphlet reproduced overleaf points out the necessity of turning the 80-mile road 'gap' into a dual carriageway to bring faster transportation to the West Cornwall Development area. Most of this is now nearing completion, and many of the photographs in this chapter show where improvements have been made along the Cornish A30 and have helped the county to prosper.

However, should the A30 be too successful, the railway could be closed, leading to an

THE ROAD TO PROSPERITY FOR CORNWALL

The Case for a
Dual Carriageway
Trunk Road

increase of 12,500 extra cars a day in the summer, plus an increase of 80 heavy goods vehicles moving along it every day.

Today, Cornwall's A30 presents tremendous contrasts. In places, for example just past Carland Cross where the windmills stand, it suddenly feels once more like part of 'the longest lane in England'. As it clings to the earth on its way between Innis Down and the Summercourt bypass it is almost like crossing heathland in East Anglia. Yet the huge sweep of the road after Indian Queens can only be a Cornish landscape dotted with mine shafts and tinners' pits, the lunar landscape of St Austell in the distance. Although I found references to photographed accidents at locations that have now been bypassed - Five Lanes, Bodmin, Lanivet, Blackwater and so on - none is shown here as a mark of respect to those concerned. The absence of accidents at these spots today must also stand as a tribute to today's modern civil engineers.

It is hard to believe that up until 32 years ago the A30 was considered by the motorist to be the main route down into Kernow, despite the existence of the Torpoint and Saltash ferries. It is an important and distinctive route and does not need to become just another European motorway from Penzance to Dover as is now threatened.

LAND'S END is where the A30 begins and ends, the start of its more than 300-mile journey to London by curving around the State House Hotel in the 'past' photo, possibly dating from some time in the late 1940s. The road still does so today, although the hotel has been enlarged somewhat. *The Land's End and John O'Groats Co Ltd*

The finger post placed inside the Land's End complex is inevitably a flimsy affair with interchangeable arms so that you can have your picture taken with your home town indicated on one of the fingers. The road behind it would have forbidden any form of transport to go any further. You could only walk to the very edge of the Kingdom. Surely this is how it was meant to be?
Devon County Council Library Services/ CCC

LAND'S END - 'the first and last fingerposts'. The cast iron fingerpost shown here is so much more fitting as a unique sign for a unique place than the standard flat Worboys signs we see today. Below the latter run the double yellow lines that forbid you to park any closer to this national monument. *Devon County Council Library Services/Author*

Opposite LONGROCK: Travelling up to Penzance and further east, the road is twisty and often congested. The volume of traffic once crawling through Longrock now passes along a new system of roads almost half a mile away, thus leaving this suburb of Penzance quieter and safer. *CCC/Author*

MITCHELL: This is another example of a village gratefully bypassed by the new A30 dual carriageway. As ever, the village is worth visiting, with its two outstanding examples of buildings boasting two-storey porches supported by pillars - the Plume of Feathers, seen here in the early 1970s and again in early 1994, and Raleigh House, back near the Pillars public house, in front of which stands the magnificently restored cast iron fingerpost seen in the third view. Up near the petrol station in the distance (£1.15 a gallon in the '70s) is a milestone indicating 6 miles to Truro. The old turnpike climbed from here to Carland Cross, were ranks of windmills now stand to take advantage of the winds on this high spot, which looks out over the Atlantic and the Bristol Channel.

Today the garage is derelict and the old road to Truro terminates with a turning space, but you can still follow the line of the old A30 as you sweep by on the new. *CCC, T. Mogford/Author (2)*

LANIVET TURN, A30: Here we see the A30 at Lanivet corner being cut back in July 1957 to improve sighting. The houses on the left are today completely obscured by trees and stand on the old road completely cut off by this widening.
Cornwall Library Services/Author

CARMINNOW CROSS, BODMIN: This ancient cross had stood on the A30 by a hamlet known as Tripey Corner (which was a little confusing as it was where four roads meet) since 1899. It is seen here in June 1975; two years later it was moved to its present position as a result of road improvements, and with the approval of 97 per cent of public opinion.

The cross's design is similar to those found carved on rocks in 700 BC at Bavian, Assyria. Hardly visible now from its present isolated position are the pit markings, which some scholars dismiss as being trivial and childish forms of decoration, and others as important since they only occur on crosses in this part of the British Isles.

Dept of Transport (2)/Neil Lindsay

BODMIN: Mr Ellis, a renowned photographer of local events, has many references in his ledgers to accidents and incidents along stretches of road that have now been bypassed, such as Honey Street, Bodmin, pictured here in February 1961. This tiny linking street ran from the High Street, through which all traffic passed, including this load from St Austell on its way to Derbyshire.

Today you will find Honey Street, opposite the church at the Launceston-bound end of the town, delightfully devoid of traffic. Pickfords is now a travel agent, and the paved area is a safe home for one of the original pillars from Bodmin Priory. *Corwall Library Services/Author*

JAMAICA INN: The name sounds as if it should be linked with *Treasure Island*, a place of heat, sand and tropical palm trees. Not in this part of Cornwall, because unlike Newquay or St Ives, where you might just imagine you are in the tropics, Jamaica Inn is in the middle of Bodmin Moor. Daphne du Maurier's tale tells how the Inn was used as a centre for smuggling gangs, and it is true that smuggling on the south coast at Polperro some 20 miles away was very big business in the early 1800s. Brandy from the Channel Islands, some 470,000 gallons of it a year, was the most famous commodity, along with linen, lace and tea. Yet when Daphne du Maurier wrote her book in 1935 she prefaced it thus: 'Jamaica Inn stands today, hospitable and kindly, a temperance house on the twenty mile road between Bodmin and Launceston.' Temperance was the last thing to be associated with such a place!

The idea for *Jamaica Inn* is said to have arisen in Daphne du Maurier's mind when she was lost in a fog on the moor with Cornish writer and scholar Sir Arthur Quiller-Couch. The heroine of the book, Mary Yellan, certainly spends a lot of time out on the moor alone.

The road upon which the Inn once stood is thought to be part of a pre-Roman road, a ridgeway route from Launceston to Bodmin - remember that Launceston was once the royal capital of Cornwall. But the course of the road across the moor has also been determined by religion and the law. The church at Temple was established by the Knights Templar in the 12th Century; Hospitallers then took it over in 1312. Launceston was the ancient capital until 1838, so this old ridgeway route had always been important.

In 1715 an appeal was made to the Bishop of Winchester to change the capital to Bodmin, at least for judicial purposes, and the request went out to 'Immediately issue warrants to or take course effectual that the roads and ways from Launceston to Bodmyn be free and the trees and hedges cut fit for travelling and coaches etc.'

However, there is no evidence of turnpiking later than this along this particular section of the A30. The coachman in *Jamaica Inn* says that it used to be a friendly place where coaches were welcomed, but that they had stopped using it because of its hostility. Today, with its extended museum features, Jamaica Inn offers a very different ambience from that which once greeted weary travellers. The welcome addition is a Daphne du Maurier room, which displays some early editions of her work along with her writing desk and other memorabilia. *CCC, George Ellis/Author*

Above Jamaica Inn today. The various inn signs since the '30s have depicted Joss Merlyn, but I wonder what hung there before. After all, brandy does not come from Jamaica. To relive the *Jamaica Inn* story you will have to abandon the roads, as the Vicar of Altarnun said: 'Roads? Who spoke of roads? We go by the moors and the hills and tread granite and heather as the Druids did before us.' *Author*

Right Winter scenes on the moor in January 1958 and January 1994. The latter shows one of the new dual carriageway sections, with the old road on the left at the horizon. Note the small sweep of the gritting machine compared with today's monsters. *CCC, George Ellis/Author*

BODMIN MOOR: These photographs, at Plusha on the way to Launceston, show the kind of improvements that were necessary from the 1960s onwards to cope with the increased traffic coming from the Okehampton area towards the honeypots of Cornwall. The road now runs straight past the farmhouse and has left a kind of 'ox-bow lake' section of the A30 to the left. The road still gives the impression of being unobtrusive as it has been dropped down into the newly created cutting. Another environmentally friendly aspect of this scheme was the use of chestnut palings during the course of road works rather than glaring orange cones. *CCC, T. Mogford*

LAUNCESTON (1): 'Gateway to Cornwall'. 'The motor age has been Launceston's main trouble. The way into Cornwall by car has necessitated a bypass. Along this are many Frank Lloyd-Wright villas; these, however, are preferable to the intrusion into the old town of through traffic.' (John Betjeman, *Shell Guide to Cornwall,* 1935/64).

Before the Tamar Bridge was built in 1961 the impatient motorist inevitably travelled to Cornwall via Okehampton and Launceston on the A30, not wanting to face the possible delays on the Torpoint and Saltash ferries.

The Southgate featured here was once plagued by traffic squeezing through in both directions, and fights over the right of way were a regular occurrence. Now after a series of bypasses Launceston is safe, although the motor bike seen racing down 'Race Hill' here could contradict that. No longer famous as Cornwall's capital, Dunheved - although there is a bridge of that name which stands on the bypass just outside the town - Launceston does have another ancient claim to fame. Most authorities state that the first stretch of turnpiked road in the country was on the North Road in 1666. However, there are records of a turnpike trust in Launceston for 1647. *Roy J. Westlake/Author*

Below Angel Hill, on the right just before the gate, was described by Betjeman as one of the prettiest streets in Cornwall. The present picture rather contradicts this. *Author*

LAUNCESTON (2): The relief for the old down of Dunheved came 20 years ago, and skirts along to the south. Provisions were made for industrial units and workshops to be retained and expanded, and so be within easy reach of the A30. However, this perhaps was not conducive to the scholarly atmosphere of Launceston College, from the gateway of which these first two views were taken, the older of which (*above*) is dated May 1974.

Looking south, out of town, Hurdon Road, across the old A30, today rises to cross the new bypass by a flyover just visible through the trees (*left*); the roof of the industrial warehouse on the left is visible in both views as a clue. *Dept of Transport/Author*

Along the new bypass towards the west is the Pennygillam roundabout. Again looking south in 1974 (*left*), first we see the B3254 just south of its crossroads with the old A30.

Today the scene is dominated by the A30 flyover (*right*), as we look down towards the new roundabout. The second, closer, modern view (*far right*) shows that the house in the centre background of the 1974 photo has survived (and its surrounding conifers have grown!). *Dept of Transport/Author*

The third 1974 photograph (*above*) shows the junction of the A30 with the B3254 (to the right), and the feeder road to the town centre (to the left). Here many houses had to go in the road improvements.

The present-day view (*right*) is looking north up the B road from Pennygillam roundabout towards the old junction - and the new flyover that replaced it. *Dept of Transport/Author*

Across the wires

The last night of the Proms is always an emotional one. The final hymn to 'England's green and pleasant land' might have been true just 50 years ago, but with man's obsession to communicate with ever increasing speed he quite happily tolerates pylons and poles in a landscape once defined by natural tree-lines and landscape features.

The march of telegraph poles - notice that we still don't call them telephone poles - followed the roads as any self-respecting army would. Before the coming of the fibre optic cable the multiple-armed pole with a single line for every telephone was, however, far uglier than what we have today. Nevertheless the sighting of these multiple-armed poles in old photographs often brings forth sighs of happiness. This can only be on account of the noise they used to make and not their visual impact. It was as if the wind became real when we could hear it as well as feel it!

Some beauty spots adopted the laying of underground cables almost from the start of the telephone boom - Clovelly in 1935, Lynton in 1938. The first long-distance undersea cable was a Cornish affair, connecting the Isles of Scilly with Sennen Cove in 1869. At Porthcurno the following year the first Empire cable was laid from here to Bombay.

Leaving the cables behind, let us take a closer look at the poles themselves. BT needs about 80,000 new poles a year and these have been traditionally supplied from Corsican pines until the introduction of the Southern yellow pine from the USA. Some poles date back to 1886 and have been found to be still sound when tested.

Instow, Devon, possibly in the late 1960s. Here we see a GPO worker up a pole, beside the then ubiquitous Morris van. He appears to be wearing neither hard hat nor safety harness. (For further views of Instow, see *British Roads Past and Present: Devon*.) *Devon County Council*

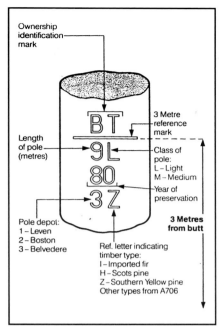

Above Dating poles can be done with the help of this information cut into them. The one in the photograph also sports a rare GPO red reflective disc. Not all the information is shown on this pole, but the diagram shows how it should be. *Author/BT*

Above right 'Why do telegraph wires hum?' asked this 'Do You Know' series card issued by Wall's Ice Cream.

'It is known that centuries ago, men made simple harps and hung them in the trees. When the wind blew, the string began to vibrate and produced a musical note. The sound of these harps, known as Aeolian harps, and the hum of telegraph wires are both due to the same cause. When the air blows against the taut wires, they vibrate at a certain rate to give a continuous musical note or hum. In a high wind the vibrations of the wire may be so strong that the whole of the telegraph pole may tremble.' *Author's collection*

Above 'Evening shadows, Polzeath.' This horrific cartoon from the 1960s shows what might have happened if the multi-armed pole had continued its march across the land. *Shell Guide to Cornwall*

Right There are still quite a few of these Post Office Telegraphs concrete and cast iron cable-joining-pit covers around. An interesting point about these covers is that if they are made of two types of material - concrete and iron, or wood and iron - they were made so as to prevent horses slipping on an all-metal surface. *Author*

Above The coming of fibre-optic cables saw the gradual phasing out of these very ugly multiple-armed poles, with their myriad fixtures and insulators. This one is seen next to a 1960s-design Shell sign, and just peeping over the wall in the distance is a pre-Worboys 'Halt at Major Road Ahead' sign. *CCC*

Below This fancy finial is just one of many that still cling to the tops of old telegraph poles. There are variations - some bear a halo round them to which were attached the multiple wires that have now been replaced by the single optic fibre poles.

Apart from these rather minor attractions on old poles it would be nice to dream of a time in the future when a book on highway monuments could be written giving one or two locations of surviving poles, which might even become listed tourist attractions. At present I doubt if anyone wants to make a hobby of spotting the four million poles in existence, and still rising! *CCC*

3. Routes south and north:
the A390, A38 and A39

'J . . . showed me where some traveller had left the expression of his impatience written upon the wainscot with a pencil. "Thanks to the Gods another stage is past." For all travellers are in haste here, either on their way home, or to be in time for the Packet.'

Robert Southey, *Letters from England*, 1802 - written in Truro

The A390 and A38

*I*n the mad dash for Land's End that often possesses many 'foreign' visitors to Cornwall, the more indirect and scenic route to their goal is often missed. This route along the south of the county was the oldest to develop, part of the turnpike being built as late as 1856 and 1880. In fact, when the great roadbuilder John McAdam was stationed in Falmouth in 1798 as a naval victualling officer, he discovered the value of Cornish greenstone for roads. It is said that he helped build the new Truro Turnpike from the workhouse out to Kiggan, now part of the A390 between the capital and Tresillian. Perhaps in the recent Woodcott developments part of his work was excavated; this new approach to Truro, with its stylish landscaping on the bends, is named after a famous coaching horse.

Today this road is being increasingly used by those seeking access to beaches and towns in the south, and it is at its junction points that improvements have been made, bypasses introduced and distributor roads constructed. Perhaps with the exception of the St Austell relief road, it is a more gentle route through the county, undulating and twisting and passing through villages that are well worth stopping at along the way.

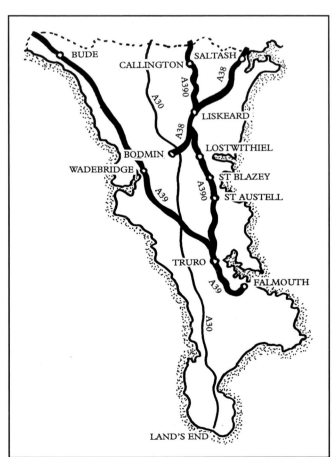

The A38, A390 and A39.

HEWAS WATER: The old A390 can be seen running parallel on the northern side of the new road in four places between Grampound and Hewas Water. This 'present' (and 'past') photograph, taken at the Trewinnow, Trevillick, turn, shows clearly the old line of the road looking back towards Grampound. Such cut-off pieces of road soon become overgrown; here heaps of conglomerate stand by the deserted road in ruins, waiting to be recorded by some unborn archaeologist. *Author*

TRURO (1): Take a look at this picture of a lorry that has crashed into the Red Lion Inn in Truro in July 1967 and you will see a lamppost festooned with directional signs - in those days all roads converged on the centre of the town. It was therefore essential to get the traffic distributed and flowing before it ever reached the centre, and the relief road achieved this and, with the addition of a 'Park and Ride' scheme now operating from the top of the Newquay/Bodmin A30 turn, Truro is now one of the most delightful towns to visit in Cornwall.

Most of the Red Lion has been replaced by a modern building, the streets are now largely pedestrianised and the only signs outside the bank are for pedestrians. *Royal Institution of Cornwall/Author*

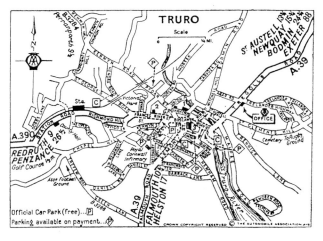

This aerial photograph and the map taken from the 1950 AA *Road Book* from approximately the same angle show Truro prior to the building of the relief road. The A39 enters in the mid-foreground, runs right through the town centre and out among the trees in the right background. The southerly relief road began opposite the junction with Green Lane just above the bottom of the photograph. *CCC/AA*

TRURO (2): The construction of Truro's southerly relief road at the junction with the A39 at Green Lane. In the first view a Foden lorry leaves the works, while another waits to cross the junction.

The 1993 view shows that the junction has been developed with a complex roundabout system, but succeeds in deflecting northbound traffic for Bodmin and St Austell on the A39 and A390 away from the town centre up the dual carriageway.

The third view shows the relief road works looking down towards the junction. This time a Thames Trader tipper is waiting to cross.
CCC, T. Mogford (2)/Author

TRURO (3): The following series of photographs shows the decline in importance for the city of parking boats, and the growing importance of parking cars. In 1944 Truro was handling 1,000,000 tons of shipping a year - after the war this dropped by half. The increase in visitors along with a decline in seaborne traffic led to many new developments in this area. The warehouses in the first photo soon disappeared, and Kenwyn Bridge was built in 1969. *Author's collection/Author*

TRURO (4) The first view is northwest across Truro River, with one of the railway viaducts just visible in the distance. In the next two views (possibly the early 1960s) the riverside warehouses have been replaced by what, rather ironically, is known as The Green car park! Amongst the parked vehicles on the left is a fine Austin shooting-brake, while on the right there's a Humber Hawk, and a fine array of motor coaches.

In 1993 the car park is softened by trees, and the garage in the background has become a market and shopping arcade. The coaches on the right are larger and more sophisticated, but interestingly there's a Ford rental van parked in both pictures! *Opie, Redruth/CCC, T. Mogford (2)/Author*

GRAMPOUND: In the widening schemes between Probus and Hewas Water that were carried out ten years ago, Grampound remained untouched, and during those ten years only the nature of its trading has changed. This was always a great market town, having its own Charter since 1383. The citizens were exempt from bridge tax, had free stands in the weekly market, could form a merchant guild and hold two fairs a year. This was a good deal. However, over the years Truro and St Austell eclipsed its success and it became notorious as a 'rotten borough'.

Today it boasts excellent Chinese and Indian restaurants and a high-class food shop along with some antique emporia. Its position on the busy A390 has helped it to survive. Unlike the A30, where rest-stops are not in villages, Grampound has thrived as old staging posts used to by providing a friendly Cornish welcome along the way. A tannery still operates in the village, and while the dairy is still present the churns are no longer with us. *CCC/Author*

As an industrial crossroads Grampound once had some importance, and here are photographs showing the tollhouse, and a milestone by the weighbridge. *Author*

ST AUSTELL: These photographs, looking west along the A390, show the junction with the Pentewan Road leading down to Mevagissey (on the left). The transportation study made in 1973 shows St Austell as being one of only three towns in the county with a bypass at that time. The bypass runs along its southern edge and once formed the boundary between the town and the countryside.

Today, however, it is being encroached upon from all sides. The garage and the junction itself have changed completely, although the White Bridge in the middle distance, so named from the milky nature of the River Austell emerging from the China Clay areas above, was built in 1926 and remains unaltered. However, with the coming of the 40-tonne lorry no doubt some strengthening will have to take place.

The 1950s photo shows a very relaxed scene with someone sitting on the seat next to the old K6 telephone box. Today you would need to wear a mask if you sat there too long, as up to 2,000 vehicles can pass by each hour. Further along the road, on the left, a clump of trees shows the entrance to what has become the Restormel Council headquarters. *CCC/Author*

ST BLAZEY (1): It is unfortunate that a town with such a holy name should have had its sanctity slightly ruffled when in 1979 highway works began in the area of the churchyard. However, it could be said that the operation was intended to lessen the forthcoming number of occupants in the graveyard. This busy junction with the road down to Fowey had bad visibility at this point, and there were then no traffic lights to slow down approaching vehicles. The rather gloomy pre-alteration photograph show a Ford Cortina applying its brakes ready for the blind corner. *CCC, T. Mogford (2)/Author*

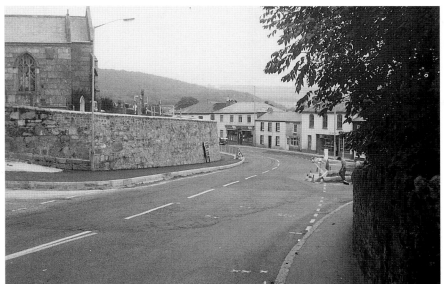

ST BLAZEY (2): As can be seen from these views of the same location, but looking in the opposite direction, the churchyard was cut back considerably. The third view shows some unfortunate removal of coffins. During the course of the roadworks flowers were regularly strewn into the churchyard. *CCC, T. Mogford*

LOOE MILLS TOLLHOUSE, LISKEARD: Today throughout Cornwall the out-of-town shopping complex is gobbling up land just as perhaps the old bypass schemes used to. Not pictured here, but something to look out for as you approach Liskeard from Plymouth past an example of the aforementioned kind of shopping complex, you will see a ruined tollhouse desperately clinging to the road and pulling its fallen slates around itself to keep up appearances.

Not so this one, pictured in 1962 on the other side of the town, then as in its heyday well placed to slow down traffic on a dangerous bend. Before the road was straightened out members of the family who ran the Looe Mills eating house on the left were forced to take Red Cross courses to help them deal with the number of accidents that happened on the road outside their door. Today the tollhouse, dated 1837, peeps out of the trees in a lay-by where the road once ran. *CCC, J. Rapson/Author*

LISKEARD BYPASS: The section of the A38 from Dobwalls to Liskeard was always a good chance to watch the speedometer climb, but once Moorswater was met, together with the town of Liskeard with its narrow streets and multiple junctions, there was bound to be a hold-up. This new bypass built in 1975 between the town and the main Plymouth-Penzance railway line involved the building of two bridges to cross the Liskeard-Looe branch line.

These photographs show where the bypass, with its carriageways at different levels, passed beneath the old road that led down to the industrial complex at Moorswater famous for its very ancient lime kilns. Moorswater Viaduct to the left, on the main line, was built in 1881, replacing I. K. Brunel's original timber-topped structure of 1859, the stone piers of which can be seen through the arches. *Liskeard Town Museum (2)/Author*

The bypass's most dramatic feature was the construction of the 12-metre-high Station Road cutting. Standing behind it, almost on top of it, is the Cottage Hospital known as Lamellion, where many elderly patients are cared for. Yet the sound of the road is not excessive here. Now that the cement structure has been in place for nearly 20 years it has acquired a pleasant pinkish tinge and its ledges are home for many rock plants including pink spur valerian. *Liskeard Town Museum/Author*

LANDRAKE: Whether or not this beleaguered village gets a footbridge is a matter for the future; all that this pair of photographs reveal to the traveller at the moment is how incapable we are of driving according to a road's circumstances. With the introduction of 'on board' computers in cars, would it not be so much better for the environment and so much more pleasing on the eye if a screen warned us of the approaching left-hand bend at 400 and 200-yard intervals?

Since 1962 Landrake has benefited by being cut off from the increasing traffic on the A38, with its three-lane carriageway and safety kerbing and traffic islands. However, when examining other bypass schemes in the county it will be noted that they have not been situated in such difficult places as this one and plenty of space has been allowed between the bypass and the bypassed. Perhaps one should rename the village 'Landlocked' rather than Landrake.

Here we are looking north. Behind the camera back towards Liskeard is the magnificent sweep of the road up to Trerule Foot on the horizon - the dips in between must have filled coachmen with horror. Equally, when looking from Trerule Foot the sight of the spire at Landrake would be uplifting for those on a pilgrimage to Plymouth. *CCC, J. Rapson/Author*

Only just over four miles of Cornwall left on the A38. *AA*

SALTASH (1): In 1952, nine years before the Tamar Bridge opened, the amount of traffic using the Saltash ferry (see pages 94-95) and driving up through the town to reach the A38 merited a major road. This residential and small shopping area was changed completely. The house in the centre of the photograph bearing the 'Liskeard Road' sign was demolished, as were the corner shop on the left and the house on the right. The only point of reference in the 1993 photo is the row of cottages in the right background, the nearest of which has since been extended. *CCC/Author*

SALTASH (2): This 1979 aerial view of the Cornish side of the Tamar at Saltash shows the road access to the car ferry between the piers of Brunel's 1859 Royal Albert Bridge for the Great Western Railway, and the new 1961 Tamar Bridge. Many readers will remember coming across the bridge and waiting to turn right along the original Saltash bypass marked by the distinctive Army Cadet's building just to the right of the roundabout.

The new bypass incorporates a tunnel under part of the town, the longest in the South West excluding Bristol. The three-lane tunnel is 448 yards in length and 10 metres wide, and runs under the houses in Deer Park, Hillside Road and Glebe Avenue; the new bypass then continues from the South Pill roundabout to cross open country, and crosses the existing dual carriageway at Larchpool. In the second view, dated November 1987, the remodelling of the junction at the end of the bridge and construction of the eastern portal can be seen.

There was some worry that the tunnel would cause delays when it came to crossing the bridge and paying the tolls, but this has not been so, and in combination with the new bypass it seems to have been a success. So why is there talk of a third crossing? *Western Morning News/Dept of Transport*

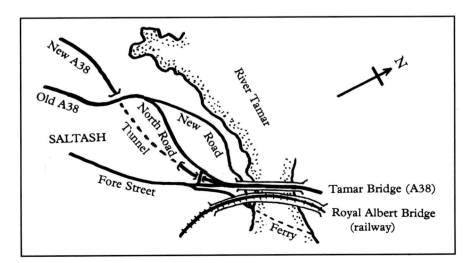

Left Sketch map showing the evolution of roads through Saltash from the Tamar crossing.

Left **Inside the tunnel during construction, August 1987.** *Dept of Transport*

Left **The western portal of the tunnel under construction in April 1987. Passing above it is the 'old' New Road, the A38.** *Dept of Transport*

Below **1993 views of the exit from the Tamar Bridge into Cornwall, and the entrance to the tunnel.** *Author*

The A39

This primary route runs from Bridgwater through Minehead and along North Devon's spectacular coastline and into Cornwall near Bude. It then runs down to Fraddon, roughly in the centre of the county, and on to Falmouth via Truro. It is known as the Atlantic Highway along with the A361 which runs north off the M5 at Tiverton. It is a road that feeds all North Cornwall's coastal attractions, the surf at Bude, King Arthur at Tintagel and old sea salts at Port Isaac, as well as the huge coastal resort of Newquay.

PLAYING PLACE (1): The final section of the A39 is curiously isolated from the rest of its northerly route. Much of it runs through deeply wooded countryside and its twists and turns slow down the driver who may have been accustomed to the straight swathes of the A390 up until now. At Playing Place one comes across a flat level area where the junctions down to the King Harry ferry stand. The site is named after the nearby Cornish theatre round, perhaps not as famous as Gwennap near Redruth, but still worth a visit. The whole junction and garage forecourt access have been greatly developed since the first picture was taken in the spring of 1983 - is that still the same lamp standard centre stage?
CCC/Author

PLAYING PLACE (2): The sight of the two cars in this early picture of the forecourt of Playing Place Garage brings the scent of wild marjoram from Cornish lanes drifting through the open window of the elegant Rolls-Royce standing at the pumps. The garage appears to have Riley and Alvis agencies, and Shell, BP, Power and National petrols are on offer.

Today's high-tech establishment is still a Shell station, but caters for quite a different volume and calibre of customers! *CCC/Author*

WADEBRIDGE (1): What is known as the Toll House Garage on the A39 much further north is actually quite a way from the tollhouse photographed here, about to be cut off from the new A39 Wadebridge bypass in 1991. The slate-hung building, dating from the 1760 Camelford, Wadebridge and St Columb Trust, now looks out towards the sea on a 'No Through Road' with its back to today's modern transport developments. *CCC/Author*

WADEBRIDGE (2): Both these photographs illustrate different disruption to highway traffic. In the first photograph we see the level crossing gates for the old North Cornwall line, in operation until 1966. Memories of Betjeman's unspoilt North Cornwall are strong here, and he would have been delighted by 'The Betjeman Centre' in the town, occupying the old railway station on the NCR's former line ot Bodmin. *Dept of Transport*

The present-day photograph shows us the traffic lights still in place at this busy junction. The 'Camel Trail' mentioned on page 73 passes across here, with cyclists and walkers on their way to Bodmin or Padstow. The old bridge is undergoing repairs, hence the disruption. But soon Wadebridge will once more be the thriving market town it always has been without any more disruptions caused by traffic problems. *Neil Lindsay*

The flame still burns

The plaque reproduced here, which is on a wall in a side street in Redruth well away from any 'enhanced area', celebrates the use of gas for lighting, not necessarily in the street, but probably in the inventor's home. It may come as a surprise to some readers to learn that gas lamps are still in use in many traditional venues throughout the country. Sugg Lighting Limited of West Sussex, who specialise in this, were first involved with the introduction of gas-lit lamps in Pall Mall in 1807. This was in conjunction with the variously spelt Mr Winzer or Winsor, an eccentric who needed to change his name quite often.

The early gas lamps were the result of the introduction of Light and Coke Companies throughout the land. However, because the early lamps had no mantles they gave out a dull yellow light. The invention of the mantle in 1885 improved matters and gauze impregnated with salts made the lamps burn brighter. Older lamps are identifiable by the fact that the top panels of the lamp were glazed. This spread illumination a little further and was also good for residents of nearby, probably oil-lit, homes.

The whole period of gas lamps belongs to the Victorian Age, hence the ornate, robust and beautiful designs that still survive in our towns and villages. Every district had its own foundry producing distinctive forms of column, and it became matter of civic and rural pride. There were also foundries that supplied street furniture to places throughout the United Kingdom - Glanfield & Kennedy of Kilmarnock, for example, whose magnificent design books are still available to view today at the Ironbridge Gorge Museum.

Today you will find lamps still burning gas in many places in London - since 1910 outside

Buckingham Palace, for example. Should you wish to return to the past yourselves, lamps for gas illumination are still available for commercial and private use. This short article gives just a taster of the many styles of lamp and column available. It is a neglected area of street furniture, but one that deserves local attention.

Finally a word about the lamp-lighter. The horizontal arms at the top of lighting columns were placed there for the convenience of the lamp-lighter who came to turn the gas on and off at appropriate times of the day. The first mention of a master lamp-lighter occurs in the Court and City Register of 1776 where one John Bird must have been expert at 'flying' from column to column. Other references to lamp-lighters always show them as running to their duties. Indeed, in the cannon of street games references are made to the lamp-lighter in different versions of 'British Bulldog', which is essentially a running and chasing game.

This lamp at Probus in Cornwall was one of the many specially built to celebrate Queen Victoria's Diamond Jubilee in 1897. *Author*

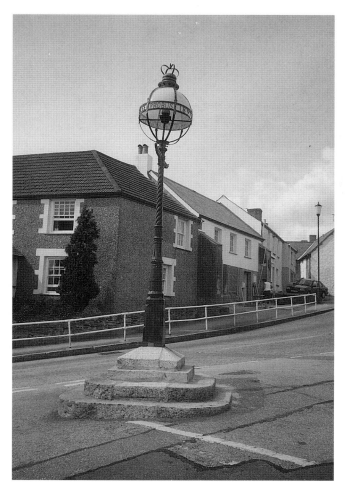

55

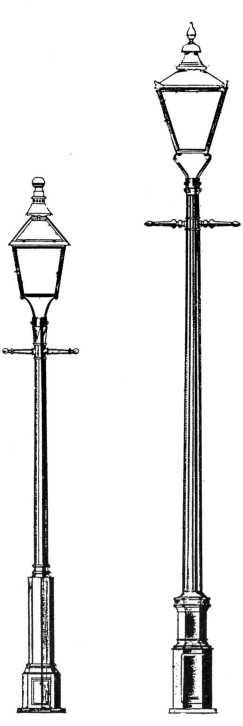

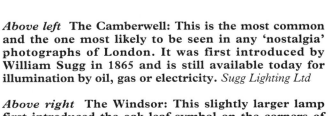

Above left The Camberwell: This is the most common and the one most likely to be seen in any 'nostalgia' photographs of London. It was first introduced by William Sugg in 1865 and is still available today for illumination by oil, gas or electricity. *Sugg Lighting Ltd*

Above right The Windsor: This slightly larger lamp first introduced the oak leaf symbol on the corners of the lanterns. *Sugg Lighting Ltd*

Left The bracket Windsor lamps shown here were photographed in Helston in Cornwall in 1977 and were installed after locals complained about the new incongruous lamps that had been fitted. *CCC*

Below The Westminster is the largest gas lamp to be found. The example photographed here at Happy Valley, Llandudno, can be verified as existing pre-1867, and there is another such lantern on the Barbican in Plymouth. These lamps burned up to 100 cubic feet of gas in an hour, and were made so large to give maximum light before the invention of the mantle, and to prevent the solder which held the panes together from melting. *Aberconwy Borough Council*

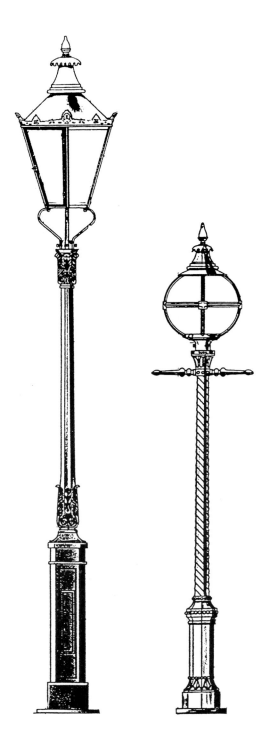

Far left The Grosvenor also bears the oak leaf emblem. *Sugg Lighting Ltd*

Left The Classic Globe: Lamps of this pattern are to be found along the Embankment in London, forming part of Sir Joseph Bazalgette's sewage and river improvement schemes. These lamps were made so that the globe could be rotated for cleaning purposes. *Sugg Lighting Ltd*

Above This delightful picture shows clearly the arm for the convenience of the lamp-lighter, and one of the variety of purposes to which the columns could be put! *Sugg Lighting Ltd*

Right Traditional craftsmanship survives in the casting and fitting of the 'oak-leaf' lantern corners to modern gas lamps. *Sugg Lighting Ltd*

Below The lamplighter. *Sugg Lighting Ltd*

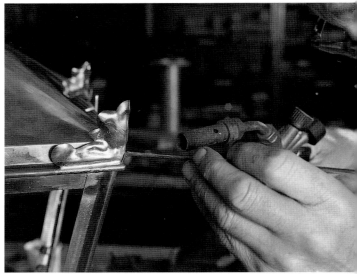

4. All roads lead seawards:
traffic and the coastline

'Cornwall is not an improvised playground; it is not a "Riviera", and the use of that word, whoever first applied it to Cornwall, was and has been a commercial "inexactitude". To any right Cornishman Cornwall is a mother with a character, a most egregious one, deferential and dear. Having that character she has a character to lose.'

Quiller-Couch's introduction to a report on Cornwall written in 1904 for the Council for the Preservation of Rural England

Quiller Couch's 'commercial inexactitude' has now become a reality. All the posters of the 1930s and '40s beckoned towards the 'Cornish Riviera', and it is a fact that Cornwall has become a holiday area very dependent on routes to the coast. John Betjeman's poem on the Duchy of Cornwall tells how the sea, angered by what it sees when it looks inland by way of tourist developments, just washes over the whole county. It leaves only the two highest points standing, rather like the story of how the Isles of Scilly were created.

I first ran away to the Cornish sea some 30 years ago. A few years later, carrying a guitar, as many did, I criss-crossed the county in a peripatetic fashion as its first classical guitar teacher. During the first few months of this adventure, because I could not drive, I was taken from school to school by County staff. It was then that I first became aware that whatever road we followed by valley to moor, from market town to stannary capital, along windy ridgeway or narrow twisting valley that in the end, as in the beginning, the story of Cornwall's roads must begin and end with the sea.

Returning to Quiller-Couch's words, given the following facts and figures one hopes that Cornwall's character will not indeed be lost. Throughout the year 3.5 million tourists visit the county, 83 per cent of whom come by car. Within the next 30 years this amount of traffic is likely to double. So many visitors come to the coastal resorts - can they take it?

Although it would seem that the seaside has always attracted children for its contact with the elements, this is not always as elemental as it could be - the boy in the blazer gets no wetter than the boy by the boat. Look beyond the latter, however, and you will see a classic family group still making sandcastles. The manufacture of wet-suits and surfing equipment has taken the place of boats and nets on many Cornish shores.
Author's collection/Author

CHURCH COVE, GUNWALLOE: This delightful cove is on the Lizard, a wild yet curiously crowded peninsula, at least at its fattest point. Setting out from Helston past RAF Culdrose is just the beginning. Goonhilly Earth Station and a cluster of windmills are seen on the horizon. Yet when you take the turn down to Church Cove the earth hedgebanks drop you back in time to the Celtic world of sea and sky. These ancient roads all over the Lizard

with their cast iron fingerposts (manufactured in Devoran) heralding the way, are best explored without a car, and this is now possible with the newly launched Discovery Trails.

Cars are the creators of many serious problems around Cornwall's 'honeypots', but the 'past' photograph here shows the triumph of the obvious. The National Trust acquired Church Cove in 1974. There was no planned car parking as it hadn't been thought necessary. But up to 700 cars were soon parking all over the beach, the towans (grass-planted dunes) and the reed bed areas. How Winnianton Farm managed to function in the summer is hard to imagine.

Now a car park, landscaped with traditional Cornish hedging, has been built to the right of the road and in front of the farm. *National Trust, D. Hume/Cameracraft, Truro*

FALMOUTH: In a county which has 321 miles of coastline it is not surprising that part of the highway authority's work should include coastal defences when their stability is threatened by the sea. The undated 'past' view of Cliff Road with Castle Drive in the distance shows work in progress when retaining walls had to be built to replace the marram grass.

Work was still being undertaken when the 1993 photo was taken, but what we now see looming on the middle horizon is the newly built Leisure Centre 'Ships and Castles'. Further on is the keep of Pendennis Castle. *Cornish Photonews, TSW Archive/Author*

NARE HEAD: Apart from the big coastal draws such as Newquay and St Ives, Cornwall's 350-mile coastal footpath sees many holidaymakers and residents throughout the year. The highways department of Cornwall County Council has this at the top of its list of current transport policies: 'To improve highway conditions in an environmentally sensitive way.' As we have seen, the National Trust also takes this view; after all, its oldest coastal acquisition, Barras Nose at Tintagel, goes back to 1897.

Almost Gunwalloe in reverse, the 'past' photograph, dated 1980, shows the obvious disruption that a car park created at this point on a farm which has belonged to the National Trust since 1931. The road could not be moved, but the farm could, as you can see in the second picture. The stone walling, although not of the traditional Cornish herringbone style, is a great improvement on the eroded hedgerows. *Both photos National Trust, Robert Chapman*

1693. PENTEWAN - JUDGES LTD.

PENTEWAN (1): The accompanying map, now nearly 20 years old, gives some idea of the growing problem of 'Caravan Saturation Areas' in Cornwall. This well-controlled site at Pentewan (in the shaded area south of St Austell), which has arrived since the earlier postcard view was taken (possibly dating back as far as the 1920s), is well tucked away beneath the cliff. A tennis court now stands where the farmhouse vegetable patch once grew, and the road sweeping round to the farmhouse has been swallowed up in other approach roads to the site. The canal which once terminated in a port here can be followed through from St Austell, and the coastal path passes behind the farmhouse and is bordered by sweet-smelling gorse and holm-bushes (a name also found in Holmbush Oak junction on the A390).

There is a convenient seat up on the cliffs here to sit and contemplate the bay. It was here that, sitting once with guitar in hand and enjoying a pasty from the shop at Sticker (now by-passed but also once on the A390), I was approached by the local policeman, who wanted to know my name and address and if I had run away from home. I was actually waiting for a lift to my next teaching appointment in Tregony. *Royal Institution of Cornwall/Author*

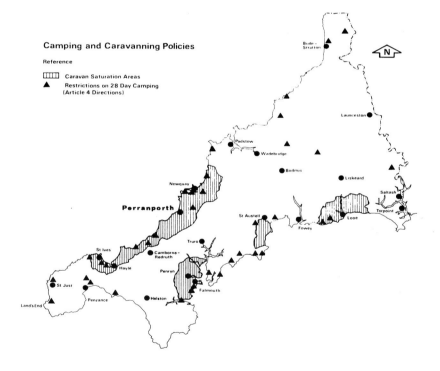

Camping and Caravanning Policies

Reference

▥ Caravan Saturation Areas

▲ Restrictions on 28 Day Camping (Article 4 Directions)

PENTEWAN (2): This scene at the entrance to the village is dated December 1955, and the improvement seems to have remained unchanged since then. The passing Morris has a Cornish - AF - numberplate. I hope that the men's footwear when working with stone was better than the rest of their 'protective' clothing. Of interest here, going towards the Mill Garage out of the picture to the left, is a gulley cover made by Oatey & Martey of Wadebridge, a strange example of foundryware from afar in an area famed for its own industrial output. *Cornwall Library Services/Author*

POLPERRO: It is from the south coast of Cornwall that the most famous tale of strangulation comes. In 1966 over 4,000 vehicles a day were recorded entering Polperro at Crumplehorn, and in the heart of the village, where the carriageway narrows to not much more than 7 ft 6 in, more than 1,000 vehicles a day were counted proceeding in both directions when nearly 22,000 pedestrians were also traversing the same section of street - a football crowd a day! The problem is well illustrated by the 'past' photo, as a Hillman Minx followed by another family car, possibly a Standard, with a well-laden roof-rack, squeeze through. What was to be done? After considering many options the only one which would work was to restrict the amount of traffic entering the village. This was the first time in Britain that such signs as 'Beyond this point only exempted vehicles permitted' had ever appeared. Signs went up at 100-yard intervals on the approach to the village saying that there was to be no vehicular access to the village centre for day visitors. Inevitably opposition arose from shopkeepers and boarding house owners, and the national press was well in on reporting the controversy.

The latest plan to hit Polperro is a 'Park and Ride' scheme - it seems that going on foot or using the horse-drawn transport provided is no longer adequate. Cornwall also has 'Park and Ride' schemes at Falmouth, St Ives, Looe, Mevagissey, Fowey and Truro. It would be a good idea perhaps to launch one from the Tamar Bridge downwards. . . *Both photos CCC*

TALLAND BAY: The hidden face of tourism. This stretch of coast along to Looe was famous for its smuggling activities, and these would have been made easier had the Admiralty mile marker boards been in position then; these 15-foot-high sheets of metal are a guide to ships testing their speed. A little like pylons and telegraph poles they have become easily assimilated into people's consciousness and accepted without question; one resident said they had always been there!

Both 'past' and 'present' pictures show the landscaped nature of this site, which has contained itself and survived to the benefit of the landscape in which it stands. Luckily, in this case the precipitously steep roads and lack of gift shops have deterred the motor car invasion. *National Trust, C. R. Clemens/Author*

LOOE: The work seen in progress here in 1956 is typical of that undertaken in many small coastal villages to prevent properties from plummeting into the road or the sea. Cornwall has the longest coastline of any county, and under the Coast Protection Act of 1949 there is an obligation to keep coastal roads safe. The county also keeps, where possible, to a.policy of repairing retaining walls in the original drystone wall styling for which Cornwall is famous. *CCC, J. Rapson/Joan Rapson*

POLZEATH: Turning now to the north coast, here are three views of this Cornish surfing beach; the first two, taken from Betjeman's *Shell Guides* of 1935 and '64, tell their own story. In this northern corner of the coast, much loved by the poet (his grave is in St Enodoc's church), surfing has taken over. The tea shops that you see as having dominated the cove in 1964 now double as wet-suit hire and surf-boarding gadgetry arcades, and the car park is still on the beach. The present photograph was taken in autumn, perhaps the best time to see this area of coastline. There is now a settlement on the north shore of the cove known as New Polzeath, and if you turn to page 31 you will see the cartoon showing how the bringing in of new services inevitably spoils a skyline. *CCC (2)/ Author*

BUDE: In operation here on The Strand in the present photograph is a pedestrian enhancement scheme, with humped zebra crossings, wider pavements and protective hand-rails, which will make life safer for all those concerned, including visitors and ducks! I mention the ducks because we hope that everything in the pollution line in North Cornwall, not just of the land-based motor car variety, will be swept well out of the way. For the past few years a huge sewage outfall project has been taking place here and is now completed. *Author's collection/Author*

The heaven above and the road below

'If man has been a country dweller for hundreds and thousands of years, he cannot, in a single century be cut off from nature without suffering harm. Holidays in the country, in mountain, hill and plain, are a mitigation of this evil, and a source of spiritual power and joy which must affect, both directly and indirectly, all the activities of the coming age.'

Dr G. M. Trevelyan, Introduction to
Youth Hostel Story, 1950

Let us leave the car behind for a moment, and take to the footpaths. When Wilkie Collins ventured into Cornwall on a walking holiday in the early 19th Century he visited Land's End and described it in sublime terms. However, he and his companion wore knapsacks and were mistaken for pedlars. Of course you would be carrying something to sell or taking something home you had bought if you were carrying a burden on your back. Either that or you were one of the countless dispossessed wayfarers who were moved from parish to parish desperately seeking work and therefore the right to stay in one place. The whole idea of walking for pleasure as a mass movement is really a very recent phenomenon.

Walking used to be as natural as breathing, a part of your everyday life - mainly to and from work, the local bakehouse, the village pump, to the woodland, to the illegal snare, to the river for poaching. Occasionally you would venture out to walk for pleasure, to church on a Sunday, or for a wedding, christening or funeral, to the pub, to play in a cricket match, to visit friends, to go courting. But for exercise's sake only, never unless under doctor's orders.

There are references to the leisure pursuit of walking in England in the writing of 18th-Century artists and poets. Bosworth and Johnson, Wordsworth and Co were given to walking about

our islands and writing about it. Women walkers were even later than men in taking to the road as a means of exercise. The main drawback for them was clothing. In the constant muddy, miry conditions their long clothes made walking heavy going. Ellen Weston, a governess, saved up to finance walking holidays to such remote places as Snowdon and Snaefell.

The first recorded walking club dates back to 1824 when 'The Association for the Protection of Ancient Footpaths in the Vicinity of York' was born. Manchester followed, then the Peak and Northern Footpath Society was formed. In London early walking groups were often associated with philosophers such as Leslie Stephen, Thomas Huxley and J. S. Mill, members of the 1879 'Sunday Tramps'!

But the real beginnings of walking as a recreational activity rather than a whim of the privileged belongs to the 1920s and '30s. The Ramblers' Association, now 74,000 strong, dates back to 1933, the year after the Rights of Way Act

The walker. This evocative illustration comes from the cover of the 1932 1-inch Ordnance Survey map series, which covered all the British Isles; it was painted by the artist Ellis Martin. Does the walker wear a knapsack or a rucksack? The difference is that a knap carries provisions whereas a ruck doesn't necessarily do this. The illustration is taken from the book *Map Cover Art* by John Paddy Browne (OS, 1990).

Above **These two seen emerging from a Youth Hostel fully equipped for their day's outing are wearing gear modelled on army equipment - canvas rucksacks and probably too-heavy military-style boots. The lady wears a skirt, the man corduroy shorts and what looks like a military-style short-sleeved shirt.** *YHA*

Right **But what did those walkers do when the corduroy and canvas got wet? All kitted out in nylon, here we see the Truro branch staff of one of the oldest providers of walking equipment, Millet's (from left to right Phil Weeks, manager, Amanda Newlyn and Greg Colman), ready for the worst that the weather can throw at them.** *Author*

was passed. Up until then, at common law, parish councils as representatives of the inhabitants at large were responsible for footpaths. This was also the year of the famous Kinder Scout trespass when walkers seeking to secure rights over open moorland as well as footpaths were sent to prison.

With over 20 per cent of the population now involved in walking as a recreational activity, the Ramblers' Association still keeps a watchful eye on your rights and since 1990 has held a 'Forbidden Britain Day' on the last Sunday in November when members locally check access to Public Rights of Way such as through farmyards - in 1993 it was through woodlands.

It seems that now, as in the beginning, we have gone back to the idea of walking with a purpose. Yet these present-day purposes could not be further from the practical ones listed at the beginning of this chapter. For example, would any of the six local men from Ham Hill in Somerset who once walked the 28 miles to Lyme Regis to join Monmouth's Rebellion in 1685 believe that their route is now waymarked and known as 'The Liberty Trail'? There are over ten long-distance footpaths and countless theme trails for the walker throughout the country. There are 3,500 miles of Public Rights of Way in Cornwall alone, and the county is keen to promote interest in their use to take the pressure off the more popular coastal areas.

Finally, a word as to why a consideration of our footpaths should be included at all in a volume on British Roads. Well, they are nearly all looked after by local highway authorities and form a major part of any county's maintenance budget. As 'Carmageddon' advances it seems that retreat into these ancient byways gives us time to consider just where we are going and where we have come from.

Photographs above and below supplied by Colin Glennie courtesy of Scottish Natural Heritage, Battleby, Perth, where a unique collection of footpath furniture, amongst other rural artefacts, is on display.

Left and above The word 'stile' comes from the Saxon 'stigilla' meaning to climb. It seems that many were put in to separate pedestrians from cattle and to stop the latter from escaping into fields where footpaths ran. Stiles come in different patterns and the Cornish one is rather like a cattle grid, stone slabs set on edge to form a barrier, the top slab being where a coffin could be rested on its way to the church; this style is also to be found in Gloucestershire. The one in the sketch is at Treslothan, near Camborne, on the footpath that leads to Troon (a village that is a must for highway history enthusiasts, as there is a fine example of an open gulley running along a row of cottages prior to the Treslothan road).

Slate stiles with holes in are a characteristic of footpaths in the South Hams of Devon - the hole was meant to trap the devil or 'thurl'. 'Squeezebelly' stiles take various forms, easing the walkers through one by one. The same can be said for the kissing gate from Broch, Berwickshire, pictured here, a more romantic substitute for a stile.

Walking in the country isn't always as straightforward or relaxing as it might sound. Take this notice board (*left*) advertising no fewer than nine trails to take - thank goodness a tea room is advertised as well!

Meanwhile, this earlier photograph (*below*) of a WD notice on the Pennine Way warns of a shelled area - 'You pass here at your own risk'. *Scottish Natural Heritage/YHA*

Above right and right These photographs show the pull of the Atlantic for recreational purposes over the past 100 years. The North Cornwall Railway, which had followed in part what was become known as the Atlantic Highway, the A39, was extended from Wadebridge to Padstow in 1899. Here we see holidaymakers arriving in July 1961 by the 'Atlantic Coast Express' from Waterloo, crossing the three-span Little Petherick Creek bridge behind 'Battle of Britain' Class 4-6-2 No 34110 *66 Squadron*.

Following closure of the line in October 1966, part of the trackbed, from Bodmin to Padstow, became a footpath, known as the Camel Trail. Here we see cyclists dutifully remounting their bikes after heeding the request not to ride over the former railway bridge. The organisation known as Sustrans, which gives such new life to disused railway tracks, is planning to link up the old lines in a continuous trail from Inverness to Dover. *Terry Gough/Author*

Below left and below To reach the Lizard, the most southerly point on mainland Britain, is now, like Land's End used to be, possible on foot. The past photograph shows the congestion that this once caused when walkers mixed with traffic. The National Trust successfully divided pedestrians and drivers, and once more created a length of wall that looks as if it has always been there. *National Trust (2)*

5. 'How many miles to Mylor?':
still rural rides

'How many miles to Mylor
By frost and candle-light:
How long before I arrive there,
This mild December night?'

A. L. Rowse

If you have seen a pantechnicon passing you on a grimy night in the Midlands with the trade advert along its side reading 'Have you tried the Lane's of Cornwall?', you would have been a brave driver to resist the temptation of doing so there and then. Cornwall has a higher proportion of its population living in rural areas than any other county. Now with the near completion of the A30 as a dual carriageway throughout the length of Cornwall

those who wish to turn off and explore the lanes can do so, but once again I would emphasise the importance of using public transport.

There are over 4,000 miles of non-principal roads to explore in the county. Given the varied nature of the terrain, the roads reflect this; deeply wooded valleys, exposed headlands, open moorland and fertile farmland, the country lanes lead to them all. For its land mass Cornwall has a large number of rural roads, but remember that towns were not a natural development but the result of speculative English feudal magnates and ecclesiastical land-owners all eager to collect rents and market dues. The Cornish themselves lived in isolated hamlets and villages, between which this mass of rural roads developed.

LOSTWITHIEL: Although this junction stands on the A390 I have placed it in the rural section in the hope that this is where it will stay. It marks one end of one of the crossover points between the main spinal highway, the A30, and the softer southerly routes; another such point is to be found at Ladock near Probus. There are no road markings in the 'past' photograph and the only sign in sight is that for Lostwithiel town on the brow of the hill. Traffic going towards Lostwithiel once fed in from the B3269 via the slip road which ran in front of the row of cottages and is now blocked off. *CCC/Author*

Right Unfortunately the present-day signs prevent us from seeing this ancient cross that stands at the junction.

There are over 300 such crosses in the county set up in the period of Saxon conquest and settlement as a defiant gesture by the Celts. This one is wheel-headed and marks the crossroads; others were praying stations on the pre-sites of close-by churches.

Halliday, in his book on Cornwall, presents an image of 'attack' from the west by the marching crosses, once again similar to the painting by John Miller in Truro cathedral:

'Imagine this host of 400 crosses gathering near Land's End where they are the thickest, as they advanced through Wedron to meet the oncoming alien near Bodmin, where, being checked, only a few - among them the noblest - broke into the eastern hundreds.'
Author

ZENNOR (1): 'Where the cat ate the bell rope and mermaids sing.' One of the great joys of writing 'Road' books is that you have to seek out places which are off the beaten tourist track out of the tourist season. So it was with the village of Zennor in West Penwith, which lies west of St Ives along the magical B3306 (marked as an 'HR' - Holiday Route - in the summer). It is the way out to Morvah and St Just, a route which has not changed in hundreds of years, apart from improvements in the water-bound and then tarmacadam surface of the 1920s, well out of our period. While these roads are too ancient to feature in this volume, they have also not changed in the last 50 years and hopefully will not do so in the coming 500. Striking back to Penzance over the Moors to New Mill one even feels that the roads are being rejected by the landscape - it wants to be free of them, and the camber rises so high that cars roll at the rebellion going on beneath their wheels.

In Zennor itself there has been one noticeable change since the 'past' photograph was taken in 1955 - the introduction of a one-way system. The road up to the church photographed here allows for traffic in this direction only. At the point where the NO ENTRY signs appear stands the 'Wayside Museum' dedicated to all that is Cornish within this field. Its connection with the wayside is that the original artefacts on display were left along the wayside by Colonel Hirst who started collecting 50 years ago.

Outside stands the Vinegar Stone on the boundary between Zennor Churchtown and the Moorlands. During times of plague, 1832-49, money which was to pass hands over the boundary was first put into the little pool of vinegar carved in the stone in order to be disinfected. *Author's collection/Author*

ZENNOR (2): Following the road up past 'The Tinners Arms' and round to the left of the church you will find the beginning of the lane that runs down to Carn Cobba House. The picture taken in 1967 shows a muddy, stony track, which must have been difficult to negotiate at times. Today, however, it has been resurfaced in a way that blends in very well with the stone walls and small fields of the area. Sand has been used, together with sandy coloured chippings, to make a firm, all-weather surface - another example of the National Trust's care in looking after its land while still providing useable access.
National Trust/Cameracraft, Truro

These cast iron fingerposts are a tribute to a county that cares about its past. They are well looked after and replicas once forged by local foundries such as that at Devoran, or the Visick foundry, now owned by the King Harry Ferry, are being made by the County Council. *Author*

GERRANS: For the motorist the Roseland peninsula is a nightmare - so best to turn it into the dream that it is and take to your feet. The coves such as Portscatho and beaches such as Towan, together with the estuary creeks such as Pelyn and Poligney, are best approached by the many footpaths and minor roads that criss-cross the area. Many of these had their origins as 'sandy ways' for the transportation of sand and seaweed as manure. High earth banks border the roads here and in the Ruan High Lanes area, and you will always find a wild flower blooming there at any time of year.

Gerrans, pronounced with a hard 'G' which belies its softness, was once the administrative centre of the area, when sea trade, smuggling and bullocks were the mainstay of the district. It was on the 1761 Creed to St Just turnpike, and we see the Turnpike House here on the right just before the church in this undated photograph. Gerrans stands just off the ridgeway route, the A3078, which runs through such unaltered spots as Veryan, Tregony and Bohartha. Note the Austin Somerset convertible and, beyond it, the distinctive wings of a Vauxhall Cresta.

The present-day photograph shows that the telephone box and the directional sign have now gone, but the fingerpost is still there. *TSW Archive/Author*

79

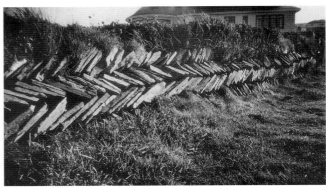

PELYNT: This is Geoffrey Grigson country, a writer who was brought up in the area in the 1930s and must have seen many a scene such as is portrayed in this 'past' photograph. Of course we can only guess at how happy, content or worn out the labourers were as they made their way up past the hotel, which is today really more of a family pub. The road has now been marked out and a petrol station appears to the left of the picture. *G. Grigson/Author*

This example of a Cornish stone wall is actually taken from the middle of the county, but it shows the characteristic herring-bone pattern of this style of slate walling. The green lanes of East Cornwall have a character all of their own, as Grigson says: '. . . the great thing about a Cornish lane is that it simulates the condition of a wood. The hedges on either side are damp, they do not get the full sun, they may even be thickly wooded along their crests.' (*The Freedom of the Parish*) *Author*

A TRULY RURAL RIDE: These four photographs were all taken on the B3254 from north of Bude to Launceston, and show the rural sweep of the road. At one point you slip briefly over into Devon, as the old decaying wooden boundary post shows. All of Cornwall's B roads are a joy to travel, giving long views over the land and nearly always a glimpse of the sea. The red-painted fingerpost stands on the 'wreckers' trail and I was told that behind it there is a mound where those who were hung on this gibbet were buried!
Author

The fall and rise of the traffic bollard

Above This scene in Shepherd St, off Piccadilly, London, shows the very earliest form of bollards in position. Well set into the pavement, they were there to protect pedestrians against horses and carriages mounting the pavement, quite a common occurrence in towns and villages. Street bollards were originally remnants of quayside furniture such as upturned cannons or mooring posts, and many in the early days were manufactured with mock cannon balls in their mouths. There has since been a blurring in meaning between the original bollard for this purpose and the traffic guard that has lately become synonymous with the bollard. The first mention of bollards in a traffic context occurs in the *Architectural Review* of 1948 and in *The Times* in 1955 when a woman is described as waiting between the bollards in the middle of a crossing. *Author's collection*

Left Pedestrian bollards come in various shapes and sizes, fluted and decorated to reflect civic pride and the design flair of local foundries. In Cornwall it is good to see that the standard pedestrian protection bollards have taken to being decorated with the county crest. These 15 bezants, gold coins first struck in Byzantium and Constantinople and showing that the holder had been in the Holy Land, represent the wealth of five of the leading Jewish moneylenders living in Cornwall in King John's time. When the King needed money to finance the wars against France they all came forward and were represented with three gold balls each. The motto, which does not appear on the bollard, also dates from this time - 'ONE AND ALL/ONEN HAG OLL' - hoping that no business decision can be made without all of the parties concerned being present. *Author*

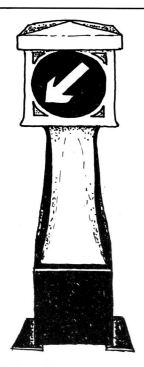

Left Waisted bollard: This design from the mid -1960s seems curiously antiquated now when we catch glimpses of it in old photographs. It still clings to the principle of the bollard as an anchoring post, more like a hitching post where horses might be tethered.

Right The design of traffic bollards was obviously in the first instance modelled on the pedestrian ones. They were waisted and constructed in two separate sections of cast iron, then sheet metal and now totally in plastic.

As far back as 1933 it seems that traffic guards or bollards were self-illuminating, and regulations concerning their dimensions were set out in the 1963 Worboys report.

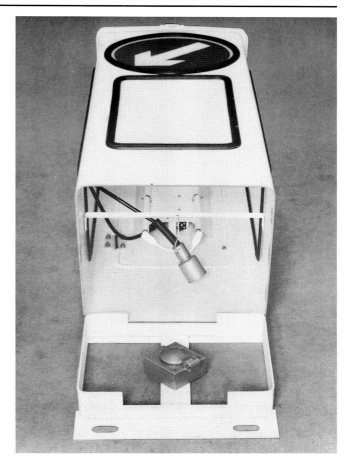

Although we are now very used to traffic islands and bollards, as recently as 1969 the first island with a bollard was introduced into St Mary's on the Isles of Scilly. Because the shape of the traffic island was very coffin-like, on the first night of its operation flowers and a cross where placed upon it. Today on the mainland one can think of islands where just crossing the road to reach them might necessitate the placing of such objects in earnest!

In the 1960s the well-established firm of Franco, which made many signs for the AA, introduced this traffic-proof bollard. At least the light fitments were likely to be saved, if not the housing. *Franco Traffic Signs Ltd*

Below Haldo have dealt with the same problem in a different way. *Haldo*

Below The Claudgen bollard: well, even such mudane objects have to be marketed. . .! *Claudgen*

6. Ferries and bridges:
hinges on the Queen's Highway

'No motor cars should be allowed on Bodinnick's nearly perpendicular hills and down its narrow streets. It is a haunted town made for sailors or pedestrians.'

John Betjeman, *Shell Guide to Cornwall*, 1935

If bridges cross the heads of rivers, then ferries cross the feet, as those of you who have walked the coastal path in Cornwall will know. There are 11 large ferry crossings in the county, but many more small foot passenger ones which really haven't changed at all since they first started operating - and that can be a very long time ago indeed. For example, the origins of the Malpas ferry near Truro are said to date back to Arthurian legend, and the story of Tristram and Iseult.

The twisting lanes that lead off the ridgeways and down to the ferries are part of that off-the-beaten-track land of Cornwall. They lead to glorious stretches of river known as Passages and Roads. Henderson lists 17 ferries alone as existing between Plymouth and Cornwall in 1934. It seems that the Cornish would rather use a ferry than build a bridge, so wedded are they to the water, but ferries are as much part of the Queen's Highway, as Quiller-Couch's daughter's story of Bodinnick shows. A doctor was called to Bodinnick late at night and found that the ferry from Fowey was closed, yet as a road he claimed it should be open any time, night or day.

BODINNICK FERRY: The ferry dates back to 1397, and in 1478 one John Davey, yeoman, was granted custody of the same. In 1720 it was purchased by Governor Pitt, then in 1834 the famous engineer James Rendell, who had just designed a floating bridge ferry at Dartmouth, put forward a plan for a road from St Austell to Tor Point, which would have done away with the ferry and introduced a bridge over the River Fowey. The cost was prohibitive and when the Royal Albert railway bridge at Saltash opened in 1859 all the ferries along the south were safe once more. Apart from Quiller-Couch's book *The Shining Ferry*, there are other literary connections.

The AA *Road Book* of 1950 gives information on the ferry as follows:

Daily service as required from 7 am (Nov to Feb 8 am) to dusk.
Subject to congestion and delay during the summer months. Not suitable for trailer caravans. Capacity 2-6 cars.
Time in transit: 5 to 10 mins.
Charges: Cars 3s 6d, tri-car 2s 6d, motor cycle 1s 6d, combination 2s 6d, passengers 3d.

The present-day ferry fares are as follows:

Car, driver and passenger £1.30; car and driver and over 1 passenger £1.35; car or van over 30 cwt unladen £2.60; car or trailer or caravan £2.60; motor cycle or bicycle 50p. Foot passengers: adults 40p, children 25p, parcels 25p.

The present ferry was built by Phillips of Dartmouth in 1963, and only a few of the buildings appear to have changed over the years in this almost timeless spot, photographed here from the Fowey side. *TSW Archive/Author*

FOWEY: Staying on Fowey's riverside briefly, this simple pair of photographs show how narrow streets in coastal villages are gradually adapted to traffic, however controlled it may be. The slipway down beside the Riverside Hotel was a sharp curve, and to allow cars and trailers to turn the wall was removed back to the lamp where the lady now stands. The phone box and seat are still in place. *CCC/Author*

KING HARRY FERRY: The Harry in question here was Henry IV and the remains of a chapel dedicated to him and Our Lady stand on the eastern bank of the Fal. This takes the ferry back to 1399-1413, but local tales of the ferry as referring to Henry VIII have always been around, as H. V. Morton records: 'I cannot stop to tell you how I left Roseland by way of King Harry's Ferry; how I heard the legend that the Bluff King (who obviously wished to show off before Anne Bolyn) swam his horse across the blue waters; or how three excited bullocks, who were taking their first sea trip, tried to sit down on a car. . .'

As late as 1889 there was a rowing boat ferry operating here, and in that year it was replaced by the steam ferry which operated until 1956. The present chain ferry, seen in the 1993 photograph, is 20 years old and is the sixth non-steam ferry to operate across the river. The 1950 AA book tells us:

Service. Weekdays every half an hour from 8 am to 6 pm (June 8 pm, July & August 9 pm)

Sundays April to September only commencing 10 am then as weekdays.

Capacity 16 cars. Time in transit 8 mins.

Charge: Cars 3s-4s, tri-car 2s, motor cycle 1s, combination 2s, trailer caravan 4s, luggage trailer 1s, passengers 3d.

Tolverne is a hamlet on the eastern side of the river on a turning down to Smuggler's Inn, and is approached once more by our old friend the concrete road. This one was built by the Americans during the Second World War and leads down to a slipway where troops and vehicles were embarked for D Day. It was visited by Eisenhower himself. In the undated 'past' view a splendid Triumph Renown drives on to the ferry. *National Trust, G. W. F. Ellis/ Author*

Hayle, from Lelant Ferry

Valentines

LELANT FERRY: The following tragic tale concerning this ferry is taken from Sir Compton Mackenzie's autobiography *My Life and Times*.

'The ferryman was a captivating figure who stood in the bows and ferried his passengers across the hundred yards of river with the power and grace of a gondolier. I see now his slanting eyebrows as he told me that autumn of a tragedy. Throughout the summer a baby seal which had lost its mother had made a habit of following his boat backward and forward each time he crossed.

'"It was like a child," he told me, "and belonged to cuddle up against me when I was ferrying over some of these furrin visitors. I asked them what they thought of my baby seal and one of they bloody visitors up and shot my baby seal. Man I don't know how I didn't throw him into the river; I suppose the Lord stopped me because if I had thrown him in he'd have drowned dead sure because the tide would have swept the bugger out to sea. I believe I'll give up the ferry come October month because I'm forever looking behind for my baby seal and you never know what I might do to the boat one day."'

The first old postcard view looks across the inlet towards Hayle, while the second shows the primitive facilities at Lelant. The ferry was never a great success and various attempts to revive it have been made and failed. With the new Hayle A30 road crossing it is no longer practically needed, but maybe someone would like to set it up again as a seal observatory!
Penzance Museum (2)/Author

The Ferry, Lelant

'In the end if we control cars and our towns and ourselves - if, if, if, but there are signs of it. This may not have to be a hail and farewell. I have that hope at least.'

Geoffrey Grigson writing in the 50th Anniversary edition of *The Countryman*, 1977

Cornwall's bridges number some 900, the earliest dating back to the 13th Century. Over 70 per cent of these are historic, being built with either masonry arches or granite slabs. They have weathered well the tests of time but will need some protecting against the coming of the 40-tonne vehicles in 1998. Other Cornish bridges were made in reinforced concrete, pre-stressed concrete and steel. However, because Cornwall is a maritime county steel structures are rare - the weather and transport problems are against them.

The most impressive series of bridges are those that span the great divide between Cornwall and Devon. There is Greystone (1439), Horse Bridge (1437), New Bridge, Gunnislake (1467), as well as Dunheved, North Tamerton, Boyton and Polson.

Early on the county adopted the policy of re-routing a road over a new bridge leaving the old one intact, and one of these is pictured below.

TREVERBYN BRIDGE: This bridge, Cornwall's oldest arched one, was first recorded in 1411 but had existed since the 12th Century. It is on the old main road from Liskeard to Bodmin through St Neot, avoiding the marshy ground of the Glyn Valley. The photograph shows the original bridge to the left and the new crossing made in 1931 where the minor road now runs. It is a blessing to think that because of the A38 and A30 developments no more bypasses of this bridge will be needed. *Author*

St. Thomas Church and Packhorse Bridge, Newport, Launceston

ST THOMAS BRIDGE, LAUNCESTON: This quiet corner of Launceston near the 12th-Century Augustinian Priory was always considered a separate entity by the townspeople, perhaps because this was where a leper hospital once stood. The bridge crosses the River Kensey on a site once forded to reach the church; in the present-day view the river is in full spate, covering the base of the cutwaters. *Devon Library Services/Author*

THE WADEBRIDGES (1): From 1468 the original 'bridge on the wool', as it is known, over the Camel served pedestrian and vehicular traffic quite well. True that it was widened once in 1852 and again in 1963, but no thought of new crossings was given until the 1990s.

These three photographs show the building of what was to become known as the 'Swan Bridge' because of its delicate structure - they would have been nicely complemented by a photograph of the pair of swans that nest just downstream of the old bridge. Instead you first see two photographs of the approach works and rock blanket across to the pier base location looking eastward across the river in December 1991. The nine piers which went into place involved the driving of 'H' piles through the river alluvium to the underlying slate. Across on the far side you can see the beginnings of the 20,000-ton reinforced granular embankment, firmly in place in the third photograph taken in July 1993.

The viaduct, carrying the A39, is 450 metres long and rises between 18 and 25 metres above the valley floor. The concrete box that you see atop these piers is 6$\frac{1}{2}$ metres wide. However, the cantilever strips at the side give a total measurement of nearly 12$\frac{1}{2}$ metres. *CCC (2)/ Author*

THE WADEBRIDGES (2): In 1991, thanks to Mrs D. Dingle, the BBC *Challenge Anneka* programme stepped in to build a new footbridge upstream over the Camel in a record three days. In these three photographs we see the Challenge Bridge just started, lit up when finished, and the view from it with the other two crossings, the old 'bridge on the wool' and new 'Swan Bridge', beyond it downstream. The Challenge Bridge bears the following inscription:

CHALLENGE BRIDGE
14TH SEPT 1991
DEDICATED TO THE MEMORY
OF KEITH BAILEY

Mrs D. Dingle

LOOE BRIDGE: This bridge, dating back to 1411, was originally only 7 feet wide and was destroyed in 1853 when the canal and the railway came along. This 1958 photo of its successor before it was widened, looking towards East Looe, shows a way with no traffic lights and some fine old cars parked along the quay on the far side.

Looe is one of several examples in Cornwall where ferries operated before or continue to operate alongside bridges. I expect they come in handy whenever bridges are closed for widening, which seems quite likely in this case with the growing popularity of East and West Looe as holiday resorts. *J. L. Rapson/Author*

A more recent (1970s?) view of the quayside at East Looe. Note the four Morris Minor Royal Mail vans lined up just over the bridge parapet, ready to rumble off down twisting seaward roads, the sound of their steady engines reverberating against drystone walls. *Dept of Transport*

Saltash – The Ferry.

Now our journey is complete along Cornwall's roads, from the Isles of Scilly to the border with Devon. Much has changed in the last 50 years, but nature has ensured that much hasn't. I hope that we continue to learn her lessons.

Left **SALTASH FERRY: This crossing had been in operation across the Hamoaze for over 600 years when in 1832 another of Rendell's floating steam ferries was introduced - the chain can clearly be seen in this old postcard view, together with two Sugg Windsor lamps on either side of the boat (see page 56). The horse-drawn 'Big Show' cart is heading back to Plymouth.**

    The system did not originally prosper here as it had at Dartmouth, but after modifications functioned right up until the opening of the Tamar Bridge in 1961. The crossing took 10 minutes and operated on a half-hourly schedule. Once the ferry boats had served their time at Saltash they were sent to the King Harry Ferry. When the last crossing was made here a family from Plymouth took a nostalgic trip across - their little boy had been born on the ferry. *Plymouth Library/Author*

Above **The former ferry buildings survive, and have found a new use.** *Author*

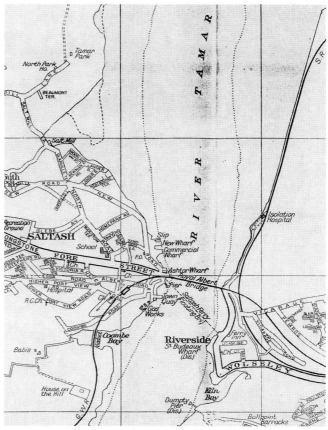

Right **A pre-war street map of Plymouth showing the way down to St Budeaux and the ferry to Saltash.**

Index of locations

THE NATIONAL TRUST'S COAST OF CORNWALL

Get to know Cornwall's unspoilt coastline with the help of a popular series of descriptive booklets. Packed with information on the history, geology, flora and fauna of the coastal land owned by the National Trust (one-third of the Cornish coast in all), the booklets also feature maps that tell you where to park, walk and find a cup of tea!

The full series is available from National Trust shops in Cornwall and from the Cornwall Regional Office, Lanhydrock, Bodmin PL30 4DE (please include a donation to cover postage).

No 1	Bude to Morwenstow	60p
No 2	Crackington Haven	40p
No 3	Boscastle	60p
No 4	Tintagel	60p
No 5	Polzeath to Port Quin	50p
No 6	Bedruthan and Park Head	50p
No 7	Crantock to Holywell Bay	50p
No 8	St Agnes and Chapel Porth	40p
No 9	Godrevy to Portreath	50p
No 10	West Penwith: St Ives to Pendeen	80p
No 11	West Penwith: Cape Cornwall to Logan Rock	60p
No 12	Loe Pool and Gunwalloe	60p
No 13	The Lizard, West Coast	60p

No 14	Kynance Cove	50p
No 15	The Lizard, East Coast	60p
No 16	The Helford River	60p
No 17	Trelissick	60p
No 18	The Roseland Peninsula	50p
No 19	St Anthony Head Battery	50p
No 20	Nare Head and the Dodman	60p
No 21	Fowey	80p
No 22	East Cornwall: Lantic Bay to Sharrow Point	60p